Sharks' Teeth And Cetacean Bones From The Red Clay Of The Tropical Pacific

Charles Rochester Eastman

In the interest of creating a more extensive selection of rare historical book reprints, we have chosen to reproduce this title even though it may possibly have occasional imperfections such as missing and blurred pages, missing text, poor pictures, markings, dark backgrounds and other reproduction issues beyond our control. Because this work is culturally important, we have made it available as a part of our commitment to protecting, preserving and promoting the world's literature. Thank you for your understanding.

Memoirs of the Museum of Comparative Zoölogy

AT HARVARD COLLEGE.

Vol. XXVI. No. 4.

REPORTS ON THE SCIENTIFIC RESULTS OF THE EXPEDITION TO THE TROPICAL PACIFIC, IN CHARGE OF ALEXANDER AGASSIZ, IN THE U. S. FISH COMMISSION STEAMER "ALBATROSS," FROM AUGUST, 1899, TO MARCH, 1900, COMMANDER JEFFERSON F. MOSER, U. S. N., COMMANDING.

V.

SHARKS' TEETH AND CETACEAN BONES

FROM THE

RED CLAY OF THE TROPICAL PACIFIC.

By C. R. EASTMAN.

[Published by permission of GEORGE M. BOWERS, U. S. Commissioner of Fish and Fisheries.]

CAMBRIDGE, U.S.A.:
Printed for the Museum.
JUNE, 1903.

REPORTS ON THE SCIENTIFIC RESULTS OF THE EXPEDITION TO THE TROPICAL PACIFIC IN CHARGE OF ALEXANDER AGASSIZ BY THE U. S. FISH COMMISSION STEAMER "ALBATROSS," FROM AUGUST, 1899, TO MARCH, 1900, COMMANDER JEFFERSON F. MOSER, U. S. N., COMMANDING.

V.

SHARKS' TEETH AND CETACEAN BONES FROM THE RED CLAY OF THE TROPICAL PACIFIC.

By C. R. EASTMAN.

(Published by permission of Geo. M. Bowers, U. S. Commissioner of Fish and Fisheries.)

WHEN, more than sixty years ago, Edward Forbes sought to explain the so-called "Northern outliers" (or assemblages of marine animals inhabiting certain depressed areas of the sea-bottom in the vicinity of the British Islands, and differing from those found over adjacent and shallower regions) as remnants of a preglacial Arctic fauna, an ingenious suggestion was put forward, which subsequently received a wide application, and has indeed been carried to unwarranted extremes in some cases.

For instance, while there can be no question that Sir Charles Lyell was wrong in declaring that "to talk of chalk having been uninterruptedly formed in the Atlantic is as inadmissible from a geographical as a geological sense," and that Professor L. Agassiz's conclusion[1] is abundantly confirmed that "the present continental areas within the 200-fathom line, as well as the oceans, have preserved their outlines and positions from the earliest times," nevertheless the generalizations once so popular, that "we are still living in the Cretaceous epoch," or that "Cretaceous outliers" are represented by the archaic types still existing at great depths, are now accepted only in a very much modified sense.

Amongst the forms brought to light by dredging at great depths in mid-ocean which have interesting palæontological relations are semi-fossil sharks'

[1] Bull. Mus. Comp. Zoöl., Vol. I. (1860), pp. 368, 369.

teeth belonging to species characteristic of the middle or late Tertiaries in Europe and America, hence implying that these bodies have been lying on the sea-floor at least ever since the Pliocene, becoming buried with inconceivable slowness by the gradually accumulating sediment.[1] Large numbers of these teeth, together with hundreds of Cetacean bones, were obtained by the "Challenger" Expedition in 1875, all of them more or less impregnated with, and their substance sometimes entirely replaced by the oxides of iron and manganese. These accumulations of vertebrate remains are not limited to any one ocean, but are most abundant at extreme depths in the red clay areas of the central Pacific and other oceanic deposits, being only exceptionally found in calcareous oozes or telluric deposits. The "Challenger" collections were described in great detail by Murray and Renard in their Report on Deep-Sea Deposits,[2] published in 1891, which was the first attempt to deal systematically with deep-sea deposits and the geology of the sea-bed throughout the whole extent of the ocean. The Mammalian bones were still further investigated and described by Professor Sir William Turner.[3]

No additional material of this nature was obtained until Mr. A. Agassiz in 1880 dredged off the eastern coast of North America a few Cetacean bones and one or two sharks' teeth from the existing sea-bed at a depth of only 333 fathoms.[4] The teeth belonged to the genus Lamna, and differed from those dredged by the "Challenger" in that the root and vasodentine remained essentially unaltered, hence implying a comparatively recent

[1] The excessively slow rate of deposition of sediment in the central Pacific since the Glacial period is indicated by the unique assortment of continental rock fragments, coated with a thin layer of manganese, which was dredged by Mr. A. Agassiz in 1899 at Station 2 of the "Albatross" Expedition. *Cf.* Mem. Mus. Comp. Zoöl., Vol. XXVI. (1902), pp. 71, 110.

[2] *Murray, J.*, and *Renard, A. F.*, Report on Deep-Sea Deposits; Scient. Results "Chall." Exp. (1891), pp. 267–276. Chapter IV. of this volume, dealing with the materials of organic origin, was written wholly by Sir John Murray. Not more than four genera appear to be represented with certainty by the sharks' teeth, namely, Lamna, Oxyrhina, Carcharodon, and either Galeus or Carcharias; and owing to their imperfect condition, accurate specific determinations are in most cases impossible. Nevertheless, Mr. Murray regards these same organic remains, together with the associated manganese nodules, volcanic lapilli, and zeolitic minerals, as "by far the most interesting result of the dredgings between Tahiti and Valparaiso." (*Loc. cit.*, 1891, p. 181.)

[3] *Turner, W.*, Report on Bones of the Cetacea; Zoöl. "Chall." Exp., Vol. I. (1880), pt. iv., pp. 1–45.

[4] *Agassiz, A.*, Three Cruises of the "Blake"; Bull. Mus. Comp. Zoöl., Vol. XIV. (1888), p. 276. *Murray, J.*, "Blake" Deposits; *Ibid.*, Vol. XII. (1885), p. 42.

burial. It should be stated that in the great majority of the "Challenger" teeth, all that remains is the hard dentine or enamel, the root and whole of the vasodentine having been dissolved away.

During the years 1887–1889 extensive deep-sea dredging operations were carried on in the Indian Ocean by English and French hydrographers, the scientific results of which were discussed by Dr. Murray in two communications published in the Scottish Geographical Magazine.[1] Among the more striking features of these investigations was the discovery by Captain Pelham Aldrich in H. M. S. "Egeria" of semi-fossil teeth of sharks and ear-bones of whales, all more or less encrusted with peroxide of manganese, as had already been observed by the "Challenger" in similar areas of the Atlantic and Pacific. The author again calls attention to the fact that two of these species, *Carcharodon megalodon* and *Oxyrhina hastalis*, are characteristic of the middle Tertiaries, and, so far as known, are not now existing.

The most recent and only other source from which this class of organic remains has been derived is the "Albatross" Expedition of 1899–1900, which forms the basis of the present report. During this cruise vertebrate material was dredged from five stations in the Pacific, whose positions, depths, and bottom characters are given in the following table:[2]

LIST OF "ALBATROSS" STATIONS YIELDING SHARKS' TEETH AND CETACEAN BONES.

Station Number.		Position.		Depth, Fathoms.	Nature of Bottom.	Number of Specimens.	
A. Agassiz Serial.	"Albatross" Serial.	Latitude.	Long. W.			Fishes.	Cetaceans.
2	3681	28 23 N.	126 57	2368	Red clay; light brown ooze.	153	15
13	3683	9 57 N.	137 47	2690	Red clay; light brown Rad. ooze.	58	7
17	3684	0 50 N.	137 54	2463	Grayish yellow Globigerina ooze.	1	0
173	3691	18 55 s.	146 32	2440	Red clay; volcanic mud.	6	0
183	3692	19 04 s.	167 41	2472	Red clay; Radiolarian ooze.	1	0
						219	22

[1] On some Recent Deep-Sea Observations in the Indian Ocean; Scottish Geog. Mag., Vol. III. (1887), pp. 553–567. On Marine Deposits in the Indian, Southern, and Antarctic Oceans; *Ibid.*, Vol. V. (1889), pp. 405–436. *Cf.* also Geol. Mag. [3], Vol. VI. (1889), pp. 514–517, Figs. 1–4.

[2] *Agassiz, A.*, Preliminary Report and List of Stations, with Remarks on the Deep-Sea Deposits by Sir John Murray; Mem. Mus. Comp. Zoöl., Vol. XXVI. (1902), pp. 1–114. *Cf.* also *Townsend, C. H.*, Dredging and other Records of the United States Fish Commission Steamer "Albatross," U. S. Fish Com. Rept. for 1900 (1901), pp. 387–562.

Comparison of Vertebrate Remains Dredged by the "Albatross" and "Challenger" Expeditions.

As the line run by the "Albatross" from San Francisco to Tahiti converges toward that run by the "Challenger" from the Hawaiian Islands to Tahiti, where the two cross, it is interesting to compare the results of deep-sea dredging accomplished on these voyages. On the run from San Francisco to Tahiti the "Albatross" made eleven deep-sea dredgings, four of which brought up sharks' teeth, as shown in the above table. On the course westward to the Fiji Islands, and thence northwesterly to Japan, three such deep-sea hauls were made, one of which (at Station 183, between Cook Islands and Tonga) yielded vertebrate remains.

Following the track of the "Challenger" from Yokohama, Japan, due east to the meridian passing through the Hawaiian Islands, and thence south to Tahiti, we find that eight stations are distributed along this route which yielded the same class of organic remains; but on the run from Tahiti to Valparaiso material of like nature was dredged at but one locality to the eastward of the Paumotu group, namely, at Station 293. The comparative paucity of vertebrate remains on the ocean-floor for a distance of 4,000 miles between parallels 30° and 40° of south latitude, as contrasted with their wide distribution and abundance elsewhere in the Pacific, is probably to be accounted for by the fact that this belt lies outside the south equatorial current, and that it has not been frequented by large sharks and Cetaceans since Tertiary times, or even longer. During the Tertiary, however, Carcharodons of enormous size ranged along the western coast of America from California to Patagonia, as is shown by their fossil remains.

Numerous Cetacean bones were dredged by the "Challenger" from the red clay in the vicinity of Tahiti (Stations 276–285), and it is regarded by Sir John Murray as rather surprising that none were in the material from the "Albatross" Station 173, which lies within the same area.[1] However, it is well known that the percentage of Mammalian remains brought up in the great majority of the "Challenger's" deep-sea dredgings was very small, and that, as Dr. Murray has himself stated,[2] "in all the terrigenous deposits

---

[1] Mem. Mus. Comp. Zoöl., Vol. XXVI. (1902), p. 110.
[2] Report on the Deep-Sea Deposits; Scient. Results "Chall." Exp. (1891), p. 270.

and calcareous oozes they were not observed." Furthermore, Mammalian remains brought up from the sea-floor are for the most part limited to bones of extremely dense structure, such as the ear-bones and fragments of the beaks of Ziphioid whales, the preservation of which is to be "accounted for by the great density of these portions of the skeleton, and the consequent small amount of surface presented to the action of the sea-water when compared with the cancellated bones."[1]

To our mind, the failure of the "Albatross" to bring up Cetacean remains at Station 173 is devoid of special significance, and does not affect the question of general distribution. More likely is the absence of such remains at this point, in close proximity to the Paumotus, to be explained as the result of local conditions affecting the solvent power of the sea-water.

The discovery of Cetacean bones by the "Albatross" at Station 2 in latitude 28° 23' N., and also at Station 13 in north latitude of about 10°, is interesting, since no remains of this nature had been previously found north of the equator, in either the Atlantic or the Pacific. With the exception of two fragments, all the bones of Cetaceans procured by the "Challenger" Expedition were dredged from red clays and Radiolarian oozes, and "these were all situated in the central South Pacific, excepting Station 160, 2,600 fathoms, in the southern Indian Ocean, 500 miles southwest of Australia."

The general facts of distribution of sharks' teeth as observed by the "Challenger" Expedition are thus stated by Dr. Murray:[2] "The distribution of the sharks' teeth in the deposits is similar to that of the bones of Cetaceans, although they were dredged more frequently. They are most abundant in the red clay areas far removed from land, and especially in those of the central South Pacific; they were less frequently taken in the organic oozes of the deep sea, and only in one or two instances in the terrigenous deposits surrounding continental or other land. It seems undoubted that many of the teeth of sharks and the bones of the Ziphioid whales belong to Tertiary and extinct species."

To facilitate comparison, and to show at a glance the distribution, the following table has been prepared, which shows the position, depth, and

[1] *Loc. cit.*, p. 276. [2] *Loc. cit.*, p. 276.

bottom characters of all the "Challenger" stations in the Pacific where sharks' teeth and Cetacean bones were obtained. At various other stations not included in this list, on the run from Hawaii to Peru, a few small teeth and otoliths of indeterminable fishes were brought up. Otoliths, on account of their dense structure and different chemical composition, are less readily destructible than other bones of the fish skeleton. Only in three or four instances were any fish bones, other than otoliths and teeth, observed in all the deposits brought to light by the "Challenger."

List of "Challenger" Stations in the Pacific yielding Sharks' Teeth and Cetacean Bones.

Station No.	Depth, Fathoms	Position.		Nature of Bottom.	No. of Specimens.		Remarks.
		Latitude.	Longitude.		Sharks.	Cetacea.	
237	1875	34 37 N.	140 32 E.	Blue mud.	Several.	0	
241	2300	35 41 N.	157 42 E.	Red clay.	1	0	Small Lamna tooth.
244	2900	35 22 N.	169 53 E.	Red clay.	1	0	" " "
248	2900	37 41 N.	177 04 w.	Red clay.	1	0	" " " [na.
252	2740	37 52 N.	160 17 w.	Red clay.	5	0	1 Carcharodon; 4 Oxyrhi-
256	2950	30 22 N.	154 56 w.	Red clay.	9	0	4 Oxyrhina; 5 Lamna.
274	2750	7 25 s.	152 15 w.	Reddish brown Radiolarian ooze.	Numerous.	13	2 Carcharodon; 9 Oxyrhina; 5 Lamna.
276	2350	13 28 s.	149 30 w.	Red clay.	250	16+	
281	2385	22 21 s.	150 17 w.	Red clay.	116	9	
285	2375	32 36 s.	137 43 w.	Red clay.	1500	50+	
286	2335	33 29 s.	133 22 w.	Red clay.	350	90+	
289	2550	39 41 s.	131 23 w.	Red clay.	1	5	Perfect Oxyrhina.
293	2025	39 04 s.	105 05 w.	Globigerina ooze, brown.	2	1	1 Carcharodon; 1 Oxyrhina.
299	2160	33 31 s.	74 43 w.	Blue mud.	0	1	Globicephalus.
					2236+	185+	

Synopsis of the Genera and Species represented in the Collection.

Of the rather over two hundred sharks' teeth dredged by the "Albatross," by far the greater number belong to the Lamnidæ, the only other family represented being that of the Carchariidæ. The five genera to which these teeth are referable with certainty may be arranged in order of their numerical abundance as follows: Oxyrhina, Lamna, Carcharodon, Carcharias, and Hemipristis. As already observed, the absence of the root and lateral denticles (in all cases where such were present) are serious obstacles to the precise identification of species, since the form and serration of the crown alone are not sufficiently distinctive characters. With the exception of *Oxyrhina crassa* and *Carcharodon megalodon*, therefore, the specific determinations must be regarded as more or less provisional. It is interesting to note that the last two species became extinct in the Pliocene.

Oxyrhina Agassiz.

Oxyrhina crassa Agassiz.

Plate 1, Figs. 11-20.

Over one hundred specimens of Oxyrhina teeth were obtained at Station 2, and about half that number from Station 13, which may be referred with little hesitancy to this species. Anterior and lateral teeth are represented in about equal proportions, the former signalizing themselves by their high and narrow crowns, not unlike those of the existing *O. spallanzani*, and the postero-lateral teeth only differing from those of *O. hastalis* in their considerable thickness. The outer coronal face is flat, the inner strongly convex, and the enamel smooth on both faces. The lower lateral teeth are triangular and erect; in those referable to the upper jaw the apex is sometimes lightly reflexed, and the crown often curved backward. All the teeth from Station 2 exhibit but a slight coating of manganese. The largest-sized anterior and lateral teeth which have been obtained of this species are shown in Figs. 13 and 19 respectively. One nearly perfect crown, much perforated by sponge borings, was obtained at Station 17, and a fragmentary one at Station 183, both belonging to this species.

This species has not been recognized as such by the authors of the "Challenger" Reports, but unnamed Oxyrhina teeth evidently identical with those here described are illustrated in Pl. VI., figs. 8-11, 13-17, and 22. Of these only the ones shown in Figs. 14-16 are anterior teeth. Although numerous specimens of *O. hastalis* were dredged by the "Challenger," the "Albatross" Expedition was not fortunate enough to obtain any.

Oxyrhina crassa ranges from the Eocene to the Pliocene in Europe, and is of rare occurrence in the Phosphate Beds of South Carolina. The latter deposits, however, contain such an agglomeration of early and late Tertiary fossils that the age of the formation is indeterminate. No good figures of this species having been published heretofore from American localities, two perfect examples are shown in the accompanying text-figures, with which the deep-sea crowns may be profitably compared. The originals are from the Phosphate Beds of Coosaw, South Carolina, and are preserved in the Museum of Comparative Zoölogy.

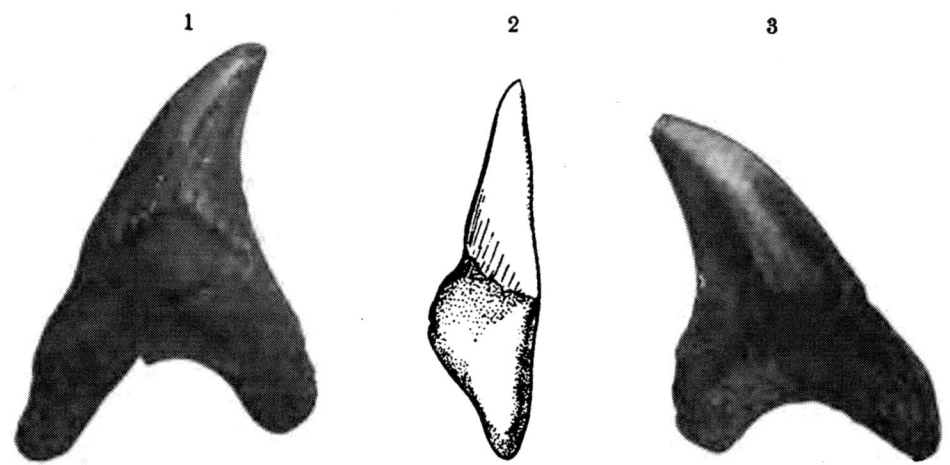

FIGS. 1–3. — *Oxyrhina crassa* Agassiz.

Phosphate Beds, Coosaw, S. C. Two lateral teeth referable to the upper jaw, one seen from the inner face and in profile (1, 2), the other showing the outer face (3). × ¾.

Lamna Cuvier.

Lamna sp. ind.

Plate 1, Figs. 9, 10.

Twenty-two slender and sharply pointed teeth were obtained at Station 2, and one imperfect crown at Station 13, which belong to a small, indeterminable species of Lamna. These teeth have the outer face faintly and the inner very strongly convex, with smooth enamel on both sides. None of the specimens exceed 1.5 cm. in height. Similar teeth are figured in Pl. VI., figs. 12, 19, and 21 of the "Challenger" Reports, and are stated to occur plentifully in the Pacific.

Carcharodon Müller and Henle.

Carcharodon megalodon Agassiz.

Plate 1, Figs. 21–23.

Fifteen comparatively small-sized teeth belonging to this species were brought up by the dredge at Station 2, and fragments of eight larger ones at Station 13, these latter being quite heavily encrusted, and their substance impregnated with manganese. The most heavily encrusted of all, however, are six large teeth from Station 173 (Pl. 2, figs. 31-33), on which the deposit of manganese exceeds 1 cm. in thickness. The largest tooth anywhere obtained is from Station 13, its crown being preserved for a height of 7 cm.

This species enjoys the same range in the fossil state as *Oxyrhina crassa*, but is more cosmopolitan in distribution. In the Tertiaries of the Pacific coast it is known to have extended at least as far north as California, and teeth either of the same or a closely allied species occur in the Patagonian formation of Chubut.[1] A tooth in the Museum of Comparative Zoölogy from the Tertiary of Aria, Peru, has a total height of 13.5 cm., and a large upper lateral tooth from Coquimbo, Chili, described as *C. gigas* by Philippi,[2] was found in a deposit which has yielded teeth indistinguishable from those of the existing *C. rondeletti*.[3] The type-specimens of several of Professor Agassiz's species of Carcharodon are now preserved in the Museum of Comparative Zoölogy.

CARCHARIIDÆ.

Carcharias CUVIER.

Plate 1, Figs. 1-6.

The large family of Requiem Sharks comprises twenty or more recent genera and about sixty recent species, the latter being often closely related and difficult of determination. In many cases the detached teeth of Galeocerdo can only be doubtfully separated from those of certain species of Carcharias. The fossil forms having the teeth in both jaws all more or less serrated are usually placed in the subgenus Prionodon (Prionace); those having the upper teeth serrated at the base only, and the lower teeth erect and entire, in the subgenus Hypoprion. The serrated condition of the cor-

---

[1] *Woodward, A. S.*, Observations on Señor Ameghino's Notes on the Geology and Palæontology of Argentina, Geol. Mag. [4], Vol. IV. (1897), p. 22.

[2] Zeitschr. f. gesammt. Naturw., Vol. LI. (1878), p. 685, Pl. XIX.

[3] *Woodward, A. S.*, On Some Fish-remains from the Parana Formation, Argentine Republic, Ann. Mag. Nat. Hist., ser. 7, Vol. VI. (1900), p. 4.

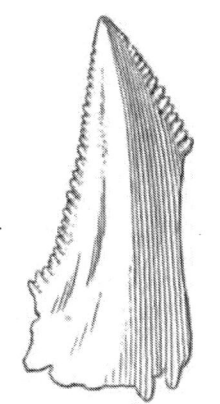

Fig. 4.—*Carcharias* sp. ind. Station 2. Outer face of same specimen shown in Pl. 1, fig. 4. × ⅓.

onal margin is well shown in the accompanying text-figure 4, which represents the outer face of the same specimen as shown in Pl. 1, fig. 4. It is evidently with the group represented by Prionodon that five small serrated teeth from Station 2 and three somewhat similar ones from Station 13 belong, but a closer identification than this appears impossible. The narrow erect teeth shown in Pl. 1, figs. 1 and 5, are evidently anterior and lower in position, and those shown in Figs. 2, 3, 4, and 6 are by the same token postero-lateral teeth belonging to the upper jaw. The originals of Figs. 1–4 are all from Station 2, and possibly represent a distinct species from those shown in Figs. 5 and 6, which are from Station 13. All these teeth agree in their considerable thickness with certain Miocene species rather than with most existing forms.

Hemipristis Agassiz.

Plate 1, Figs. 7, 8.

This genus comprises several Tertiary and one still living species, the latter being an inhabitant of the Red Sea. The teeth are readily distinguishable from those of Galeus, Galeocerdo, Carcharias, and the like by the peculiar denticulation of their coronal margins. In Pl. 1, figs. 7 and 8, are shown two teeth belonging to an unidentified species of Hemipristis, both from Station 2. An enlarged view showing the serrations of the coronal margin is given in the accompanying text-figure 5. Two Hemipristis teeth were also obtained by the "Challenger" Expedition, and are figured in the volume on Deep-Sea Deposits, Pl. V., figs. 10 and 11. Figs. 8 and 9 of the same plate are probably of Carcharias teeth.

Fig. 5.—*Hemipristis* sp. ind. Station 2. Inner face of same specimen shown in Pl. 1, fig. 8. × ⅓.

TELEOSTEI.

The solitary evidence of bony fishes from the deep-sea deposits obtained by the "Albatross" is afforded by a small scapula brought up by the dredge from Station 2. The paucity of fish-remains, other than teeth and otoliths, has already been commented on as a striking fact, the explanation of which is probably to be sought in their different chemical composition and lesser density.

CETACEA.

Relatively few Cetacean remains are contained in the collection, fifteen specimens having been dredged at Station 2 and seven at Station 13. With the exception of several unrecognizable fragments, these consist of the tympanic and petrous bones of dolphins (Globicephalus or allied forms) and Ziphioid whales. The tympani and periotics usually occur in the detached condition, but in one or two cases they remain fused. None of these bones attain the size of the corresponding elements in *Globicephalus melas* of existing seas, and no large tympani of baleen whales, such as were obtained by the "Challenger" Expedition, are represented in the collection. Owing to lack of material for comparison, it is impossible to make more than approximate determinations. Several of the better preserved ear-bones are shown of the natural size in Pl. 2, figs. 25–29. In Pl. 1, fig. 24, and Pl. 2, fig. 30, is shown a peculiar bone of small size and dense structure, with three projecting prongs, which may perhaps be regarded as a Cetacean incus.

EXPLANATION OF PLATES.

PLATE 1.

(All figures are of the natural size.)

Figs. 1–4. *Carcharias (Prionodon)* sp. ind., Station 2. All of these specimens are seen from the inner or convex face; the original of Fig. 1 is an anterior lower tooth, and the remainder are postero-lateral teeth referable to the upper dentition.

" 5, 6. *Carcharias (Prionodon)* sp. ind., Station 13. Inner face of an anterior and an antero-lateral tooth of a small species possibly distinct from that illustrated in Figs. 1–4.

" 7, 8. *Hemipristis* sp. ind., Station 2. Inner face of two much decomposed crowns.

" 9, 10. *Lamna* sp. ind., Station 2. Two anterior teeth of a small species seen in profile and from the inner or posterior aspect.

Fig. 11. *Oxyrhina crassa* Ag., Station 2. Inner face of a small anterior tooth.

Figs. 12, 13. *Oxyrhina crassa* Ag., Station 2. Inner face of two large anterior teeth.

" 14–18. *Oxyrhina crassa* Ag., Station 2. Average-sized examples of the postero-lateral dentition.

Fig. 19. *Oxyrhina crassa* Ag., Station 13. Inner face of a large specimen belonging to the lateral series.

" 20. *Oxyrhina crassa* Ag., Station 2. A rather heavily encrusted lateral tooth corresponding in size to the anterior teeth shown in Figs. 12 and 13.

Figs. 21–23. *Carcharodon megalodon* Ag., Station 2. Rather lightly encrusted lateral teeth.

Fig. 24. Supposed Cetacean incus from Station 2; also shown in Pl. 2, fig. 30.

PLATE 2.

(All figures are of the natural size.)

Fig. 25. Right petrous bone of *Globicephalus* (?). Station 2.

" 26. Left tympanic and petrous bones still retained in natural association and apparently referable to *Globicephalus*. Station 13.

" 27. Left tympano-pteriotic of *Globicephalus* (?). Station 2.

" 28. Left petrous bone of a Ziphioid whale. Station 2.

" 29. Left tympano-pteriotic of a Ziphioid whale. Station 13.

" 30. Supposed Cetacean incus, also shown in Pl. 1, fig. 24. Station 2.

" 31. *Carcharodon megalodon* Ag., Station 173. A comparatively large-sized and very heavily encrusted specimen.

" 32. *Carcharodon megalodon* Ag., Station 173. A lateral tooth having a moderately thin coating of manganese on the outer face, and a very thick deposit on the inner, which presumably lay uppermost.

" 33. *Carcharodon megalodon* Ag., Station 173. A lateral tooth evidently buried in reverse position to that shown in the preceding figure.

PLATE 3.

Track of the "Albatross" from San Francisco to Yokohama.

"ALBATROSS" TROPICAL PACIFIC EX. SHARKS'TEETH   PLATE 1

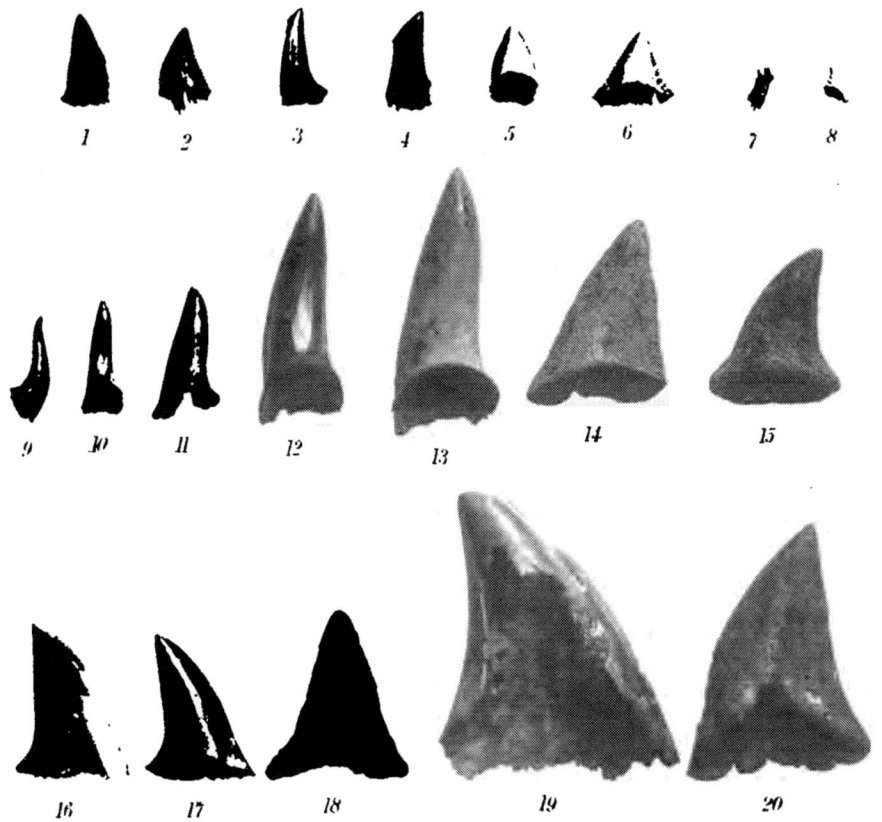
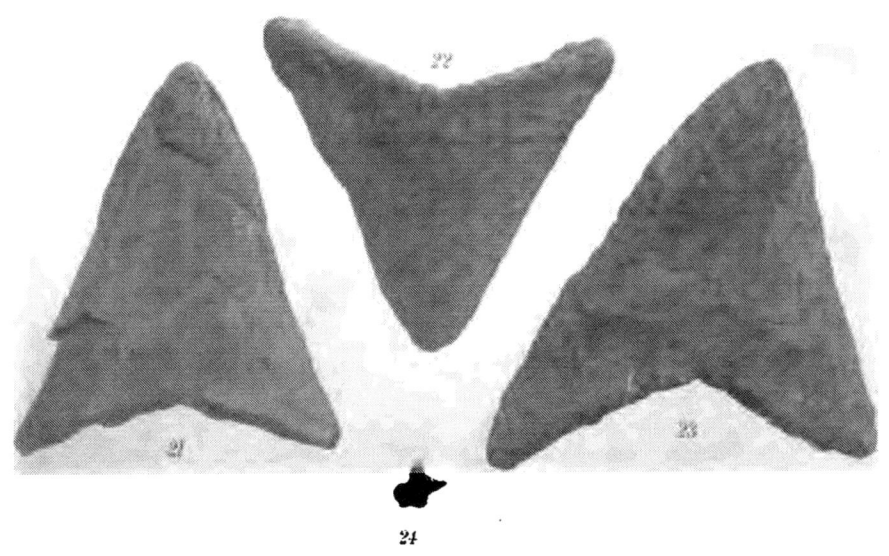

"ALBATROSS" TROPICAL PACIFIC EX. SHARKS' TEETH

PLATE 2

Printed by Libri Plureos GmbH in Hamburg, Germany